THE SKY THAT DENIED ME

MODERN MIDDLE EAST LITERATURES IN TRANSLATION

Series Editor
Dena Afrasiabi

Other titles in this series include *The Fetishists* and *The Black Rose of Halfeti*

THE SKY THAT DENIED ME

SELECTIONS FROM JAWDAT FAKHREDDINE

Translated by ***Roger Allen*** *and* ***Huda Fakhreddine***

CENTER FOR MIDDLE EASTERN STUDIES
The University of Texas at Austin

Printed in the United States of America

Library of Congress Control Number: 2018956068

Cover Design by Sam Strohmeyer
Book design by Allen Griffith of Eye 4 Design

Translated from:

Hadīqat al-sittīn (The Garden of Sixty), Riad El-Rayyes Books, Beirut 2016

("Birds of Poetry" "A Poem . . . or Something More Beautiful" "Another Prose Poem")

Fusūl min sīratī ma' al-ghaym (Chapters from my Life with Clouds), Riad El-Rayyes Books, Beirut, 2011

("One Day We May Recall . . ." "I Found Only Myself" "Leaves for Many Falls")

Laysa Ba'd (Not Yet), Riad El-Rayyes Books, Beirut, 2006

("You" "Splinters" "Pasttime" "My Enemy and I" "Winter Evening")

Samāwāt (Heavens), Riad El-Rayyes Books, Beirut, 2002

("Heavens")

Manāratun lil-gharīq (A Lighthouse for the Drowning), Dār al-Nahār, Beirut, 1996.

("The Sky that Denied Me" "Winter Words" "Birds of Regret" "Bird")

Lil-Ru'ya waqt (A Time for Vision), Dār al-Dār al-Ādāb, Beirut, 1985

("Violations of Physics")

Awhām rīfiyya (Rural Fantasies), Dār al-Ādāb, Beirut, 1980

("Things Lost" "Insults" "Rural Fantasies")

CONTENTS

INTRODUUCTION

JAWDAT FAKHREDDINE was born in 1953 in the small village of Sultaniyeh in south Lebanon. He maintains that the sources of his poetry are an intimate conversation with the Arabic language and a childhood bond with nature. His early formative readings in Arabic poetry and the landscape of his southern village, together, form the space of first encounters and discovery which continues to inspire his poetic language.

He belongs to the second generation of Arab modernists. In Lebanon, he is sometimes included under the label "Poets of the South" (*shuʿarā al-janūb*) which circulated in the late 1970s and early 1980s. A probable justification for this grouping is that the poets all hailed from villages in south Lebanon and their poetry, in an earlier period, addressed concerns and challenges of life in southern villages, especially the ongoing resistance to the Israeli occupation. Many of the poets themselves reject the label today and find it reductive and unrepresentative of their varied poetic projects.

Fakhreddine's work maintains an urgent conversation with the Arabic poetic tradition. He succeeds in translating the voices of his Pre-Islamic, early Islamic, and Abbasid forefathers into the contemporary moment. His more recent work exhibits a departure from familiar territory. Hitherto strictly a verse poet (*tafʿīla*), Fakhreddine has composed two prose poems (included in this selection: "A Poem . . . or Something More Beautiful" and "Another Prose Poem"). Whether in prose or in verse, Fakhreddine's poetic language is simple and refined, yet guided by subtle tensions which transform the mundane, the domestic, and the everyday into poetic linguistic events.

He has published more than ten poetry collections and was awarded the Sheikh Zayed Book Award in 2014 for a collection of children's poems. He taught for over forty years, most of which were at the Lebanese University. He is also the author of many articles and critical studies and has published two books of literary criticism.

THE SKY THAT DENIED ME

BIRDS OF POETRY

for my daughter, Huda

1. The birds of poetry come,
sidling toward my heart.
Their range is far removed,
yet my heart is their approaching skies.
The wings of distance are but rubble and relics,
echoes of songs are dry,
like blood on camp-ashes.
Here, I am the sound of desert wastes,
cavalier of stray language.
I relish meaning,
a gazelle walking over the desert, wounded,
thinking there is refuge with me . . .
but as it approaches,
it sees only danger and wasteland all around.
When I gesture to it, it vanishes from my sight,
leaving me like a passion shunned.
Yet it leaps over time
as though it were time awakened
when all around me the eyes of creatures
have dimmed and a night, like death,
has enveloped them, leaving me

alone in a darkness from which even secrets flee in fear
and desires are crushed.
How can I not rue its loss,
that gazelle of fancies cast away by the deserts?
How can I not raise myself
when the birds of poetry come to me?
I wonder how they come to me,
sidling toward my heart as they alight.
There is no horizon . . .
Horizons here are tombs and ravens.
The wings of distance are but rubble and relics,
yet the birds of poetry still come to me!
So do I mourn everything around me,
Should I be confident or bewildered
as I rise toward myself?

2. A time has passed
with us living in these homes, our homes;
it is they who have abandoned us.
Maybe, after losing a people in us,
people who founded those homes on their longings,
On passion or defiance,
In pebbles, sand, trees, and rivers,
along rugged pathways,
by day and at noon.
Between staying and leaving there is no difference,
if homes are homes.
What of us? Are we moving?

A time has passed as we went from
the traces of one ruined abode to another.
For us, all sense of staying and leaving is now lost.
The houses, our houses, have cast out our loved ones with no hope;
They have cast us out too,

and moved on.
Maybe they came back to meet us and our loved ones,
there in our ancient odes,
perhaps they went searching for passions
melted on the sands of yearning in their corners.
Perhaps they went searching for horses
that inscribed the names of riders on soil
every day when their corners gleamed . . .
Homes have abandoned us,
with us still inside them.
They have abandoned us.
Perhaps they were annoyed with us;
after being a firmament, they turned into prisons.
Perhaps the stories we made up and told for centuries bored them.
Maybe they waited ages for us to replace them
for our new journey.
Such a futile wait left them scornful;
they had no choice but to leave us.
A long time has passed
and the homes, our homes, have abandoned us,
then left us behind as shadows
in the very shadows they cast behind them.
We started calling it a country,
and that word "country," as the dictionary tells us,
may be, through its people, a home,
and it may be so without them.
It may be simply soil.
The country, our country, has become a wasteland.
There may be more of us,
and yet it has turned into wasteland.
So then, how can I not rue that gazelle of meaning
which has now become a crippled phrase.
All meanings have entered the catacombs of lexicons
and never re-emerged.

Even so, there are still opportunities for a leisurely stroll
through our odes both ancient and new.
All meaning is always part of meaning
because poetry always violates dictionaries,
stirring up pearls of language formerly hidden,
because poetry never seeks refuge in a nest;
instead it flies,
so that the language that winnows it in its nests may prosper.

Whence do the birds of poetry come toward me?
From which far-off places?
Maybe they were omens; no matter.
poetry only brings good auspices;
every one of poetry's birds is a good augury.
In its flight it comprehends the earth's regions, the earth's winds,
a space where the earth becomes chaff.
What then do I say to the ruins we call homelands?
How can I weep for them?

Can I weep for them when poetry's birds are still coming to me?
How can I when the wounds' echoes and the meaning's gazelle
still seek refuge with me?
How would it be if I invited into the poem the homes I have lost?
Would the home itself recapture what it has lost in us?
How nice if homelands could live like meanings in poetry.
How nice if homelands could depart like meanings in poetry.
How nice if homelands were like the gazelle of meaning,
without homeland,
shrinking and running off.
It then devises its glances
lavishing the magic of its eyes on its surroundings . . .
and it keeps wandering,
wandering without limits.
It knows no limits to its vagaries,

to its enjoyment of such vagaries,
to passion.
If only the birds of poetry could scatter my days,
turn them into drizzle so as to wake the ruins,
give shelter to countries,
and light to homes.
If only I could doze off,
to be woken again by auspicious birds
sidling toward my heart.
If only I could forget, then the birds of poetry could release me in search of the gazelle of meaning.
Maybe I could then recover a shadow of every aspect of desolation
or find once more an echo of my voice in the wilderness.
Death is all pervasive,
neither night nor day passes by along the roads.

(Beirut 2016)

A POEM . . . OR SOMETHING MORE BEAUTIFUL

1. I told my wife, now that we have reached sixty together—
with myself a bit ahead of her,
we will be living from now on
the most wonderful decade of our lives . . .
After that we will be in our seventies—
with me a bit ahead of her.
Again we will live the most wonderful decade of our lives.
Then we will be in our eighties.
At that point every year will be an added gift,
a fate like those that have guided us ever since we met
like two joyous, oblivious children.
All this I told my wife . . .
and what is yet more wonderful
is that she agreed.

2. We used to suffer from two illnesses:
I from my obsessions
and my wife from an illness that lurks in the bosoms of women.
She was stronger than I and made light of my fear.
Because she was stronger, she was completely cured.
As for me, well, I too,

maybe,
yes, I too was cured.

3. We were happy with ourselves,
whereas before we had no idea that we were happy or how . . .
But now, over thirty-five years later,
we have come to appreciate happiness.
We can test it and live it both length and breadth.
And so we have started being happy with ourselves,
as we were,
without knowing how happy we are or why.

4. When I keep one of my stories hidden from her,
I feel something missing,
I feel that what I am hiding makes me hollow,
makes me empty.
But what restores me to myself every time
is that she sees through me,
worrying about what I am hiding.

She both knows it and does not know.
She makes me clear in my own eyes
as though I had never concealed anything
or kept any of my stories hidden.

5. In my eyes, she is both morning and evening;
for my fingers, she is both sunrise and sunset.
I have only chewed my fingernails on occasion
because I lost track of her (before I knew her)
or was oblivious of her (when we met)
or was distracted from her (when I knew her).

6. We walked under the rain,
there in a distant land,

under a single umbrella.
Small trees would envy us,
and lofty trees.
In the distant land, we did not dissolve
nor did we feel like strangers.
We used to see strange faces, strange roads.
We would reward our illusions
and keep walking under a single umbrella . . .
Wherever we went, trees followed us.

7. When we first met,
we jumped to our tomorrow
and there we began putting our days in order
and living as one remembers . . .
Now that is how we are still, walking together.
Every day the morrow is our starting point.

8. The garden of our house is not yet complete
in our village that we are still composing.
Whether from near or far
we are still composing it every day
so that the world around us may be shaped by our passions.
In our passion then is the awakening of creatures,
Our passion is the ecstasy of becoming.
How then can our garden be complete?!

9. We only like to travel together.
. . . and we have traveled a lot,
But only once . . .
Since we met . . . and forever.

(Beirut 2014)

ANOTHER PROSE POEM

1. My share of women is very small,
maybe because I have forever striven
to keep myself for myself.
My share of women is plenty:
my wife . . . and she alone.

2. My share of disputes is big
because I see faults sharply.
My share of friendships is also big:
my wariness and solitude
and lofty trees that grow in desolation.

3. My share of morning is small
for in it I find sleep sweet.
My share of evening is also small:
because I love in it that which resembles me,
and yet evening has no patience for me.

4. My nature is as distant as deserts,
as meek as gardens,
as timid as roses about to wither.
My nature is defiance . . . hidden,

defiance shackled inside me.
My nature is not here
but in remote distances,
out there,
a welcoming, expansive nature
stretched out beneath a confused or begrudging sky.
My nature is like oblivion
like immortality.
My nature is sitting like an oak tree
and standing like a cypress.
Part of my nature is breaking apart after standing strong,
punishing myself when I am wronged,
and rewarding it when I am forgetful.
I often sit with myself,
in order to wander in its unknowns.
It remains resistant
like virgin nature.
My nature involves waiting for the beginning of seasons,
to gloat at their ends,
yet still fear the beginning of seasons.
. . . Perhaps I have always been ignorant of my nature
and unaware of my share in it.
Do I live in quest of my share in it?
And how then can I be
(if but once)
true to my nature?

(Beirut 2016)

ONE DAY WE MAY RECALL . . .

to my father in his absence

1. On your own now with no fear;
leave fear to me.
On your own now with no despair;
leave despair to me.
Yet you have bequeathed me the nobility of your fear,
the purity of your despair.
Your pains are no more,
and yet I cling to them in the hope of making my way toward you.
Disease crushed you,
and yet now you have escaped its clutches.
Your pains gone, you are cured.
I have not been cured,
but I am getting stronger,
as though we were sick together.
I have been trained by the disease that crushed you.
Now death has come closer than any idea that taunts me;
it is as though you have bequeathed me everything of you
that is missing,
the strength crushed by disease,
your fear, your despair.
You can rest easy because I have become stronger.

Sleep peacefully.
Your tomb is now your fortress.
Sleep peacefully with no fear or despair.
Leave fear and despair to me.

2. For your illness there was no doctor.
In fact you used to think I would treat you.
Every time you would seek me out to ask:
"What do the doctors say?"
If I said nothing, you would believe me; you would relax
when my words reassured you.
In the hospital room, on that final day,
as you squandered final glances in surrender,
I heard you whisper: "Don't leave me."
I wonder, did I let you depart on your own,
or now you are dead, can you feel my presence and
nestle beside me?
Is it you who have treated me, I wonder,
or I who have treated you?
Even though it was you who were sick, I used to nestle beside you.
You made me aware of myself,
and drew me closer.
And now your departure has given me clarity.
How then could you say to me: "Don't leave me"?

3. Once they washed away your poisoned blood,
the labored breathing quit your chest
a shudder spread to overwhelm you.
But then you felt reinvigorated.
"Shall we go home?" you asked me.
"Let's see what the doctors say," I replied.
You believed me and dozed for a while.
When you awoke, you apologized
because you had gone home without my knowing.

4. Now I have your watch;
it has stopped.
It still keeps good time,
stopped just as it has.
After a month of fighting the illness in your hospital room,
you would ask me: "How is time doing?"
Then you would ask me again: "How is time doing?"
You started accelerating time,
eager for it to pass without account.
So you handed me your watch,
as though you were giving me a time that remained
for a faded vision
Your body collapsed, and its pulse fluctuated.
You handed me your watch,
as though you were charging me with keeping your pulse
going afterwards.
So here I am now, my pulse throbbing,
keeping track of time bit by bit,
seeing your hour at every turn.

5. Tomorrow, when we meet again,
one of us will realize that we have never separated.
How then shall we meet?

6. Two companions we were,
and now even more so than before.
You returned to me strong
as though in death you left behind the disease
(for a while it had beset us).
You shook it off and were free of it.
You returned to me strong.
Now you are close to me;
like me you grieve and rejoice,
like me you are happy and annoyed;

like me you hesitate when I ask you:
"Are we going forward or backward?"
How are we proceeding?
Is our tomorrow our yesterday?

7. You used to ask me:
"Do you see our shadow, I wonder, still standing in our ancestors' garden,
strolling for a while in the morning
and again in the evening?
At noontime it may well seek shade amid our trees and disappear."
I would respond to your question:
"One shadow or many?
Doesn't each one of us have his own secret?"
Then you would whisper to me:
"Ours is a single and only secret,"
even though you always reckoned that many shadows (indeed fresh shadows) crafted our ancestors' garden every single day.

8. You were always afraid for me,
walking beside me.
People depressed you,
and you chose to look on me as a refuge for yourself.
More than once the earth kept us apart;
many times it seemed to you that I had gone far away.
Whenever you were alarmed,
you would draw me to you in sheer devotion.
You would worry about me and stay close,
despairing of those who opposed me
as though you could only see people as impeders;
you were never good at people's games.
You were alone, and would see a crowd bending over,
swinging to and fro in a vast wasteland.
So afraid were you for me
that you looked on me as a refuge for your own lost hopes.

9. A lightning flash used to traverse our village sky,
sheltering in our dreams as they danced in vines that had
embraced our steps for centuries.
I would see you watching it, holding my hand.
You knew I would be following a flash that toyed with us in the
shade of those vines.
You worried I might come to grief from temptation or strain.
You took me into the care of your hands,
the care of the words you turned into a gleam
that glistened wherever we headed.
With your hands you took care of me,
with words that seized us like a lightning flash traversing
our village sky.
In our house poetry was stars in the sky;
when we were up at night, so were they,
and they would stay there awake while we paced afar.
You took me into the care of your hands,
with words that resembled our steps.
You used to look into words and treat them with affection,
releasing them into the sky where the lightning flash would
dazzle us.
In our house poetry was the yearning of a child
staring up into the heavens.
I would see you, always watching me.
You worried I might come to grief from temptation or strain.
. . . and you realized I would be following a flash that dazzled me.
You took care of me from afar,
worried about not seeing me.
So you were always with me,
embracing my falls,
watching my every move,
holding my hand.

10. Together,
on a day that is to come, we may recall

the evening shadows that embraced the sessions we held,
that brought us together in a time whose beginnings are now
lost to us,
with a few of our friends,
in a corner of our ancestors' garden.
On a day that is to come, we may recall
the sky's shadows that embraced a sense of friendship,
fostered by poetry,
a sense that emanates endlessly in a time whose beginnings
are now lost to us.
On a day that is to come, we may recall
the sky's shadows that embraced a time
which came to stand near us on one side of our ancestors' garden.
One day we may recall . . .

(Beirut, Summer 2010)

I FOUND ONLY MYSELF

1. I found only myself,
so how did I disown me?

2. I used to see everything as short;
the poplar would accompany me
like a long-time brother;
we would walk together on the morning that deceived me,
then walk together in the evening that I did not deceive.
Our third was the foggy shroud that embraced us and snuggled between us . . .
From the start the poplar used to understand me,
understand me and see my confusion;
when I stumbled, it was taller than me,
whenever I thrived, it was a bit shorter.
But, like me, it was skinny and brittle,
and in it harm burrowed.
Maybe I am its shadow,
maybe it is mine.
Together we roam;
It is haunted by every obsession
that haunts me.
It is the poplar;

it has kept me company,
wandering with me through gardens of fleeting dreams.
We revealed a delicate pride
as we fearfully surveyed the family's tree.
The poplar,
light of pride, secret of elegance,
and, whenever it takes wing . . . eloquent speech.
The poplar,
The secret of our friendship is that we resemble each other timidly,
embracing our solitude in the heights
and harm within us leaves its scars.

3. I used to see everything as small.
Night took me roaming,
gave me space so it could observe me,
and sat me close to one of its windows so I could see beyond it.
In childhood it had embraced me
and closed my eyes to distances that cried for help,
offering me its pearls, the fruit of my loneliness.
after that it grabbed my hand and moved ahead,
taking me round.
Behold, the ground was fear of the gazelle,
cradle of mirage, echo of songs.
Grabbing my hand, it moved ahead,
and lo, imagination was closer than a trench in the road,
further than a flash in the sky.
It took me ahead, and the earth enveloped me.
There in Hadramawt it paused;
it let down fresh veils,
it stretched out for a while to catch its breath.
Now heavenly portals loomed before me,
enclosing a valley in whose wilderness
the waters of prophecy were still sheltered,
and low trees were still shaded with a tender love.
Mimosas they were, having grown in poetry's soil;

I found them roaming along paths sketched by fate.
I walked there for a little on my own.
Night wanted me to find my path,
so it released me into the sky enclosing Hadramawt,
but just when it was rushing to leave again,
it took pity on me.
Mustering its resolve
and taking my hand,
it grasped me--as in childhood . . .
and pushed me ahead.
With its robes rubbing against me,
I walked on.
And suddenly the land is
the gazelle's fear,
the cradle of mirage,
the echo of songs.

4. I used to see everything as few,
so poetry told me: this is my way.
Whenever you proceed, you must always search for it,
always lose it,
see it and not see it.
So then you have to roam with me
. . . and we set out . . .
Poetry was the companion and the light,
it was the call close by
and the call far off,
it was longing, perdition, resurrection,
it was the unruly heavens at times,
it was the liberal heavens at others;
it was both defiance and tranquility,
it was the transparent and the concealed,
it was mountains and plains,
it was there in everything,
it was dust,

it was time created between the fingers,
it was place dissipated like ether,
it was shadows and suns;
it was my path to myself,
guiding me whenever weakness or despair led me astray.
In it I would see myself renewed,
I would see myself hesitant.
It was my path to myself,
and I was my path toward it.
I still submit myself in its presence so I can appreciate myself.
. . . In it I could see myself roaming, stumbling, intensifying,
I would see myself as a youth, a child, an old man.
Through it and in its presence I used to feel life enhanced,
more prolific as day followed day.
Through it alone and in its presence I can see time,
feel it, toy with it, saying: Have confidence in yourself.
Do not grieve over your pointless persistence;
if you so wish, reminisce a little,
and, if you so wish, enjoy your forgetfulness.
O time, do not lose heart in boredom, loneliness, or hunger.
When poetry toys with you, you should be content with yourself.

5. I found only myself . . .
and here I am proceeding,
seeing everything as short,
everything as small,
everything as few . . .
As I walk, I ask myself: I wonder, have I disowned myself?!

(Beirut 2007)

LEAVES FOR MANY FALLS

1. Leaves grab the street,
   carry it away,
   and do the rounds.

2. Leaves grab the street,
   erase it,
   then rewrite it,
   painting it in many colors.

3. Here tree-leaves
   ripen like fruit
   blown by the wind.
   They float on horizons colored time and again.
   Various days on a single day,
   various fall seasons.

4. How is it trees come out in fall
   and produce such colors?
   How is it that fall is wedding celebrations
   where trees are decked out . . . only to be stripped bare?

5. Here tree-leaves are a garment that the street takes off,
then wears again,
a garment that the wind first weaves,
then tears apart;
a garment for a space that is neither created nor destroyed.
Here tree-leaves are a dust storm
that restores a spirit that has roamed
ever since the world began.

6. The sun is capricious,
but the trees treat it the same way.
The game of colors is a fixture between sun and trees.
It is the leaves that play the game,
but the sun is the one always defeated,
dwindling into patches,
fleeing like scared gazelles,
scattering pearls of confusion amid the branches
and tree-roots.

7. I walk along this street or that,
here and there along streets without number.
I follow colors . . . colors follow me.
Leaves toy with me, making me like a feather.
Here are leaves for countless streets,
leaves for countless fall seasons.

8. I walk along this street or that,
here and there along streets erased and rewritten by leaves.
They told me: Some of the forests here are virgin . . .
How many leaves have the trees here expended,
how many colors!
I keep walking
and say: I wonder, has anyone ever passed here before me?

9. In cities embraced by trees
it is the trees that shape and obscure them.
Does mankind seek a companion other than trees?

10. I adopt trees as my companion and walk.
And lo, the street walks too,
following us bewildered . . .

11. One of the trees spoke to me: Come closer.
So I moved closer,
One of them asked: Do you know me?
I hesitated,
and one of them stretched out both its arms.
Then I sank a little
as I paced among the trees.

12. Ah me! If only we had a history,
not written by ourselves,
but by the leaves on trees.

(Bloomington, Fall 2007)

YOU

When others are effaced
and I alone stand tall like a fresh poplar,
when night descends like a membrane
and my window sighs like a solitary star . . .
when memories or hopes take me,
the river hails me beyond the gardens,
secrets speak about me in the dark,
and I spend the evening alone,
resembled by songs that shine
from far, far away.
When I am on my own
and poems come to me,
leaning over me like shadows,
and the magic of their edges touches me;
when this happens . . . and more,
you are here,
and we are together,
where there is a fresh poplar and a window,
where there are gardens with a river behind,

and night,
and secrets speaking of me in the dark.
It is you then, nothing but.

(Beirut 2006)

SPLINTERS

1. ***Path***

A path to our house in the South
trodden frequently by wars.
Each day we repair it,
and over it we repair our lives
so as to continue the pattern of wars.

2. ***Heavens***

The sky emerging from the hell of terrors
has never risen.
It has fallen into the garden
and scattered like broken glass.
A storm of bombs hurled some windows
into the garden soil.
A star shivers in the hedge
which has become like the horizon.
The hedge is now like the limits of the sky.

3. ***Fig***

The fig tree . . .
It overcame our despair, every time.
Its fruit used to turn yellow if it noticed our fear.

The fig tree, the garden's very foundation,
its leaves wither.
The garden's roots are spawned from its base.
It is the summer's joy,
carrying it and wandering with it in daytime
and whispering in its ear at night,
stirring its breezes . . .
The fig tree, the garden's basis, its joy . . .
When the bombing started,
it cowered, not saying a word.
Then it gestured at summer
to disguise itself like a vagrant amid the fields.

4. ***Bee***

A bee alighted close to a pot of faded flowers.
The buzzing erased by splinters
murmured like a thorn over the soil.

5. ***Fog***

To whom did that fog speak?
The fog of the vales that breathes at dawn?
To whom did it speak when it came
and the face of villages became clear, sunk deep in the ruins
of houses?
Does it make its way, I wonder, among those ruins?
Does the groan of houses, now shriveled like embryos,
reach its ears, I wonder?
Did it lose its way amid the alleys,
trying to dissipate, but unable?
A fog that squandered directions
and faces of villages
is now crushed amid the ruins of houses,
crushed and throttled like dawn in the vales.

6. ***A Balcony***

A balcony rocked by the tempest
hardly able to stand the terrors it witnessed.
And yet it remained stolidly in a place with an overlook.
From there the plain loomed, and the night,
and violated trees and grass that resists every turn.
There loomed also fear, misery, and despair;
renewed hope in every fear, in every despair.
Everything now loomed, yet it saw nothing.
There it stayed from where it could look down,
fluttering at shadows, branches, birds,
staring out at the plain between east and west,
and at the night between sunset and sunrise.
No plain is plain; no night is night.
Everything loomed for it, yet it saw nothing;
it simply kept on looking out and fluttering . . .
A time passed it by, destroyed by wars,
so it rose
and swam in the clouds of war's savagery . . .
A balcony scared of the tempest,
yet it remained stolidly in a place with an overlook,
stolidly in a time destroyed.
It kept on overlooking, fluttering, rising
in case some new time might touch its lofty desolation.
A balcony surveying life,
then moving upwards in a distant moment.

(Beirut 2006)

PASTIME

1. I divide my time into two halves:
   one I try to grab,
   the other I toy with, then lose.
   All I grasp, then, is the lost half!

2. Between one sky that goes
   and another that comes
   there is only a yearning summer
   and clouds . . .

3. The white bird has returned.
   It came yesterday
   and hovered close by,
   white, white, oh so white!
   Now here it is, back again today,
   coming closer now and hovering close by,
   closer and closer and closer.
   Whence comes the white bird?

4. The phone rang,
   issuing a warning on the balcony
   where I sat alone.

I assume that I am gazing toward the ends of the world
beyond the distant horizon shrouded in loaded clouds . . .
The phone rang
and woke me up.
Then came my friend's voice,
informing me that the operation had to be done,
a day or two . . . it would be done,
open-heart surgery.
But my friend reassured me,
"Nothing to worry about," he told me,
"It is now a common operation."
How should I respond?
Now here he is again,
reassuring me from his hospital room,
while I sit on the balcony amazed,
assuming that I am gazing toward the ends of the world
beyond the distant horizon
shrouded in ashes like clouds.

5. From my lofty spot
did I see something amid the tree branches,
at times the plain before me,
at others the valleys and a few hills?
here and there trees bursting forth
like one or more chance encounters,
resting quietly,
swaying in exhaustion,
or rushing . . .
A clear space it was,
clasping the scene from beginning to end,
while I have no idea: am I seeing something calling to me?
Did I used to see something, like me or my thoughts,
resting, or swaying, or rushing?
Did I see something amid the dazed branches,
or was it I who was swaying on my own

in my lofty spot above the scene,
above the plain that was somewhat agitated,
so to me it now resembled my thoughts,
trees on hilltops,
or trees in valleys?

(Beirut 2004)

MY ENEMY AND I

1. If I have no enemies,
   how can I face myself?

2. I fight my enemy
   in cold blood.
   I don't fight him at all . . .
   that way he dies slowly.

3. My enemy who haunts me
   can die of sheer fury over there,
   where I shall never be ready for him,
   a place where, scoffing at what has befallen him,
   I leave him to wrestle with his deception in peace.
   My enemy who haunts me
   can do whatever he pleases and haunt me as much as he wishes.
   I shall never be ready for him.
   I shall leave him
   to wrestle with his deception in peace.

4. My enemy who deserves that I confront him
   is my own invention.
   He knows how to surprise me.

5. I confront myself with myself,
and so
my only enemy
is my delight in revenge.

(Beirut 2004)

WINTER EVENING

to Salah `Abd al-Sabur

1. Late at night you come, returning
as though you were a light late for sunset.
You return to spread some of your dreamy torments
over the ruins you have entrusted to us.
Now you return to us
because you are still waiting
while signs from the unseen world have not yet arrived.
You still wait where you are,
your death being your wait's redoubt,
your death the tower of a winter evening where you
have withdrawn.
There you are stronger,
and your dreams can proceed where you wish.
However, those signs from the unseen world have not yet arrived.
So relax a little,
rid yourself of that prolonged insomnia.
Let us stare at night's end
when you come like a light late for sunset.

2. I have seen you in the unawares of winter,
you who in winter die alone.

I have seen you listening to rain that does not pour,
limpid like despair shining behind the clouds.
I have seen you as serene as a new clarity.

3. I have seen you in a shudder of evening,
you who die alone in the evening.
I have seen you alight on "the trees of night,"
Embracing the secret of sunset like a star moving toward its cradle
or searching for itself in a distant space.

4. It is as though I feel you now
gleaming behind the winter
in which you have died alone;
now traversing that evening
in which you died alone.
You are returning to us as you have always been,
simple, sorrowful,
speaking as though you live in silence
and, as you speak, attracting silence.
You are returning to us as you always have been,
shattered, close, powerful,
that you have always been just as you said.
You were shattered, you were close by,
and now here you are,
gleaming through the seasons.

(Beirut 2002)

HEAVENS

1. The nether heavens chase my illusions
gathering the trace of my steps in the soil;
bewildered they take it back on high.
I do not believe them . . .
Instead I proceed, treading
over a wasteland burned by yesterday's suns.
I ask my illusions for guidance,
and my wandering pulls me along, befriending the distance.
I do not believe these nether heavens . . .
what I believe is every aperture brought by winter;
I believe the gleam robbed of its allure by winter's falsehoods.
With the eye of the wave I can glimpse that wasteland, discarded
in the face of the suns of its loneliness . . .
have frayed and risen every day . . .
my gaze looks to it for protection,
spread-eagled in every direction.
In it I walk, led by my illusion,
comforted by my doubts.

2. Neither night confides in me,
nor daytime's expansive face.
By day I accompany the nights' echo,

then at night I go with some echoes of daytime,
repeating the tune that takes my days to the horizon of melancholy
and choosing my longing for my language which I forever seduce;
it lures my puny flares in order to enfold them,
The suns of my days, then, rise to the embrace.

3. A language,
the dawn which for me casts the nets of a first love,
a language,
the wilderness that I have fraternized,
a language,
the passion I live;
it carries me, haunts me;
I fear it as it does me.

4. In my footsteps the river sleeps,
and the desert rises in my gasps.
From my loneliness, I draw the spirit of trees,
building my tiny heavens just as the trees' heavens are built.
I hurl my shadows into the desert wastes
and force the unseen river to flow wearing my shadows;
it is the river where the clouds of my dreams pour down,
the river that steals away like secrets, wearing my shadows.

5. In the house are trees and a sun,
and the family heavens never sleep;
they stay awake to guard our slumber
and stay alert to protect our wakefulness.
Often they draw near to touch our silence;
whenever stars of our vision burst forth, they rise up and up;
no screens confine our heavens;
they approach and soar with no limits or screens;
at every moment, they excite us with a window, then another . . .
and a door.
These heavens are close in their distance,

distant in their closeness;
in them the sun is our yearning for remote climes,
and beneath them the trees are only some of our concerns.

6. They have soared like signs of fresh winter,
Racing to the gates of clouds
as though they were a lightning flash of my longings
that I have kept hidden throughout the seasons,
as though they were my voice that I have kept sheathed in
some secrets of speech,
as though they were my secrets.
I tell them,
my children who have soared like signs of fresh winter:
you are neither any of my secrets,
nor are you my defiance.
You are the zeal that I cannot contain and which contains me.
Do not be my impetuous self;
you are your own visions,
the heavens that pour into my soul and swim in my blood.
Whenever vision seizes me, you are my distant heavens;
you are the river's prayer in my silence and my language.
So always be yourselves,
be like the joys of fresh spring,
Racing to the gates of stars.

7. I grant the clouds my misgivings,
and they lead me through the gullies to peaks of desire.
I choose only my misgivings,
where narrated tales are mere trifles, conjectures.
I take refuge in my misgivings;
they are my paradise--no, my hell,
They are the corner I choose,
The corner that rises like oblivious towers
I grant the clouds my misgivings
so their clarity will not go astray amid mankind,

so they will remain hidden, concealed like pearls.
I take refuge in my misgivings,
and then, my chest is like the cloudy sky.

8. Of my time, all I've gained are its remnants setting in gloom,
of my time, I've only gained its remnants,
stammering between foreboding and dream.
I do not know whether I have balanced its plenty with its paucity
and considered that I have captured its length and breadth.
Yet all I have of my time is its remnants!

9. No! You are not abandoning me,
because you are where I rise up,
where I slumber,
where each day I light a candle or two
from my burning zeal which I still water with blood.

No! You are not abandoning me,
because you are where I look,
where I listen,
where each day in the corners of night I search
for clouds to which I can surrender my tomorrow.

No! You are not abandoning me,
because you are where I am strong,
where I am weak,
where every time I feel the light
slipping between my fingers like one aghast.

No, poetry,
wait!
No, you are not abandoning me.

10. Passion is a reckless arrow
aimed from me and at me.

So do not say it is something frivolous affecting us both;
it is aimless,
but it is from me and at me.
Do not suggest that we are twin arrows; rather a single one.
We are not one,
and yet we are not more than that.
Do not say . . .
What do we have left of everything we have said?
It is passion that yields to me,
toying with my days,
eluding me.
It is passion that I have aimed elsewhere, yet it hit me.
It is reckless,
from me and at me, at you, from me, from you.
We are not one,
and yet we are not more than that.
so are we living a mere frivolity that sweeps us both away?

11. Death: is it enough for me to raise my flag over the earth
and to say here is my drift toward the skies.
Death: is it enough for me to raise my flag over the earth
and to say here is my journey at an end?
Death: is it enough for me to discover the heavens
which have lived with me?
Death is not enough, says a cloud wafting for a moment
over the lake's edge,
say the waves of lakes that have grown dark,
say the meadow grasses.
Death is not enough, nor is life.

12. The nether heavens chase my illusions,
calling to me and panting behind my illusions.
I walk on, not believing them.
I confide in the desert larks as they rise in the tranquil expanse,
so the hills quiver.

I walk toward the regions of my silence,
chock-full of inner thoughts,
as lonely as prophets resorting to their own silence.
I do not believe these nether heavens,
and yet the distant heavens will carry me.

(Beirut, Fall 1999, Winter 2000)

THE SKY THAT DENIED ME

The sky that shaded me in the morning,
I felt in the evening, having denied me.
I stood beckoning to it, but it did not approach.
I sat on a balcony of sunset shades.
But it did not come closer.
But I sensed it,
and I went to it far, far away,
and I reached to embrace it
after it had left me alone on a balcony of sunset shades.

(Beirut 1996)

WINTER WORDS

Winter and I,
when it comes, it does not find me.
I am late for a meeting that we set one day.
It is time, but I am always late.
Winter and I . . .
It arrives, but I miss it.
I only know its greetings
for whenever it comes, it leaves a few words,
drizzle, blame, and a new promise.
I gather what I can, though I am afraid of tears,
for I have learned a few of winter's words.

(Beirut 1996)

BIRDS OF REGRET

Am I not he who is visited from time to time
by birds with feeble wings?
Am I not he who takes refuge in remote illusions
whenever visited by the birds of regret?
He retreats a little,
surveying his feckless illusions,
illusions that to his eyes seem like illness?
Am I not he . . .
who returns to himself
and sleeps in the hope of sleeping,
yet is visited by the birds of regret?

(Beirut 1996)

BIRD

1. The heart tells lies.
   From it heavy beats plunge into the pit of this body.
   The heart tells lies,
   and a lightning flash and lengthy shivers radiate
   to the farthest limbs.

2. The heart plays, it does not lie.
   It plays, pulsing amid humble organs.

3. It is the heart then,
   the little bird of this body.
   Frolicking in its pit.
   Beating there,
   Still hovering wingless in the chest's cavity,
   Bumping against its own echoes,
   choking sometimes,
   coy like shy words,
   yet lofty like noble secrets.

4. It is the heart
   that will fall asleep tomorrow.

Will a bird manage to escape this body's cavity,
a bird which, beyond these dried up skies,
knows other cooling skies?

(Beirut 1995)

VIOLATIONS OF PHYSICS

1. ***The Law:***
   It barks,
   seeing like a blind man,
   scuffled by echoes that howl,
   by insects.
   It waves its rags,
   twisting like breaths dissipating.
   Things are confused,
   but it remains upright,
   seeing like a blind man
   barking at the chaos of things.

2. ***Time:***
   A person
   at ease, biting his fingernails,
   never forgetting; in fact, chewing on something burning.
   A person,
   the speeding days
   trip over his hands,
   fall over his feet;
   he spots them rushing hunch-backed and lame.
   He extinguishes his gaze and resorts to the warmth of his fingers;

is he claiming that in them there is something that blossoms
or that raves?
At ease, biting his fingernails,
never forgetting; in fact, he hears something bending.
He forgets his eyes,
and delights whenever he sinks into the chair like a scared cat.
Is he claiming that a drizzle falls on the mind?
How often has he thought that his assertions are not idle?
Sometimes it happens that in a moment he discerns
a life being repeated;
sometimes it happens that he longs for an opportunity
for repetition.
How often it happens,
how infrequently it happens.
Now here he is, about to tighten his grip
on dust being renewed.
A person,
smoke has settled over his eyes
smoke that drowns the keen eye.
A person,
at ease, biting his fingernails,
forgetting his eyes.
So he stares at days as they flee,
days rushing by, hunch-backed and lame.

3. ***The Fall:***
Where a void exists,
all bodies fall as though empty.
Where space exists,
bodies are confused
and fall into fear.
They move up or down,
swimming in the horror of their own punctured composure.
Why the fear?
Does the falling body not plunge out of love?

Is it pursuing anything but the arrow of failure?
Why the fear? Falling is a declaration.
The exhausted body falls ill
in order to recover.
The love-sick body falls into thirst
in order not to be extinguished.
The sleeping body falls into temptation, pleasure, pain,
all in order to wake up,
and the alert body in order to be distracted . . .
All the symptoms are alike,
so the deceived masses fall into regret.

4. *Death:*
Every morning life is opened wide for us.
In sleep, we take off a life that does not rise again.
Then we say: "We have risen again."
One of us is pushed by the other,
One of us clings to the other.
Eyes intertwine,
hands intertwine.
Gazes are a firmament that fumbles about,
words an encounter that trips.
Nothing is seen or clutched,
nothing save suspicion,
save a language embracing illusions.
They are the people:
they sail the hazardous seas of their insights,
reaping one veil after another,
incurring toil,
and chasing shadows that resemble them.
Rarely do they pay attention to steps that flit around;
they notice an impact
where their tread has no ground,
where their realities are seized by sleep or neglect.
How can they sleep when their eyes remain in the wind?

They are the lost vigil,
the insane journey.
They are the people:
Every morning when life is opened wide for them,
they say: That is life, so let us ravage each other.
(People are asleep. When they die, they take notice).

(Beirut 1980)

THINGS LOST

What we lose,
how can we know, as we remember, what happened to it?
Does it stay lost?
How cruel if it comes back to bite
at a gap that it has left in the mind,
coming like a person searching for something lost,
sneaking in,
slipping away,
disappearing . . .
maybe not coming back.
What does it do in its absence?
Has anyone come across something lost?
Does it think about places to live or jobs to do?
Does it play?
Forget?
Lose?
Look for what it loses?
What does it do in its absence?
Is everything lost collected together in some country?
Some time?
Does it think?

Does it shatter
or vanish?
Sometimes I sit,
sit for memory.
Everything lost comes back: burdens and worries,
only things lost.

(South Lebanon 1979)

INSULTS

We insult,
and think that insults comply,
going where we intend.
What a useless intent!
How can any one of us be insulted without intent?
We are insulted,
and we are good at remembering insults.
While we forget
we still keep remembering them,
we even get to like them
for fear that they might disappear into
a void of vengeance like a fading star.
In our hearts, we nourish their illuminations
so that the insults may remain a spirit,
searching for tranquility
within the folds of our despairing outbursts,
so they may remain an outburst that rocks our arid tranquility,
remain as pain,
the commission of pain,
a wasteland like no like;
so that for us a serene and simple homeland may be created,
sleeping and dozing content,

and getting up oblivious to death's gaze,
then moving nimbly . . .
until a serene homeland may be created for us
safe and simple,
unobserved by fear.
But we preserve our lurking fears, being so good at insults!

(Beirut 1979)

From RURAL FANTASIES

1. ***At the Entrance of my Village***

I arrive penitent; will you welcome me?
I was none other than your small child
led astray by time.
Whenever he strayed, distance led him even farther.
When he returns to you penitent,
you make him a lover.
Will you welcome me,
as though I am your last visitor?
How can I not be overjoyed?
How can I not become a lover?

2. ***Autumn Sun***

Burning with hatred
. . . hidden by clouds.
But, as though exhausted, it returns
to dispense an imaginary fury.
Apart from trees, who else can understand this sunny disease?
They strip away their verdant dress
and weep naked!

3. *The Fig Tree*

It makes cracks in the house floor, telling of a caving in to come,
reaching for a space that never comes closer.
As time goes by, its yearning for an imaginary sky leaves it sleepless,
planting roots in the soil to crisscross down below.
In summer (when the sun sports a searing nudity)
it provides wonderful fruit.
How difficult is this fig-tree,
as though its sap were a hectic blaze?
In our village people acknowledge that the fig is the most luscious fruit,
and that, when the trees wilt amid vines,
they do not depart; they weep.
What would happen if all the fig-trees went away?

4. *First Rain*

The soil is an extinguishing,
heavy ash that dies like a prolonged wait
. . . then is surprised by a first rainfall.
A longing now returns to it like growth
and its breaths release an odor of beginning.
These are the songs of water flowing;
it is the beginning of creation.
What aroma wafts from the earth's sighs?

5. *The Chair*

In the middle of the street is an empty chair.
The street keeps silent watch over it.
Around it hover neglected worries.
A mirage comes and goes, despising passers-by.
No one sits on the chair,
and the street remains baffled.

(South Lebanon 1978)